"THE ONE IN THE POCKET"

Break free from the "love habits" you are stuck in and unlock the relationships you deserve.

BY: JENNIFER 'MIZ J' PRIMOUS

Prelude

I'm not a psychiatrist, or relationship therapist. I'm a woman who, like many others, have found myself in a common place that requires an uncommon antidote. Although I studied psychology for four years at a prestigious college and achieved a number of specialized certifications, my true-life experiences with the help of collected data and research, are solely the fuel that sent me on the journey to discovering my truth.

Like most, when faced with a harsh reality, I went on a quest to find the answer to a question that began to fester in my thoughts and even reactions to the most simple life situations. I couldn't watch a movie or even attend a summer concert without being haunted by glimpses of happy couples and me surrounded by a pack of other singles fondling the same thought: "Why am I still single?" It was like opening Pandora's Box.

Once I got closer to the answer, even more questions began to arise: "Why do I always attract the SAME type of men?" "Will I ever get married?" and the ultimate: "Does TRUE LOVE really exist?" Like most women, and men, I found myself singing the same song and moving quickly into a cycle of confusion, anger, depression, a library of highlighted and marked self-help books, and ultimately bitterness. It seemed to me that what I was taught and believed about love and relationships, for most of my life, was all a fairy-tale and somehow it was now my responsibility to find the truth…no matter how much it hurt.

The journey didn't take as long as I expected yet it brought about all of the emotions I anticipated and more. I found myself as a young adult caught in the "dating game"; sizing up my opponents and counting down until the final round betting on who would be the last man standing. I even developed a system to sustain my perceived success in love yet it wasn't until a "TKO" that I saw my name engraved in the loser's seat. I'd been dancing around so much that I became delirious to the blows I was taking and numb to the pain of all my failed relationships. So, like most, I locked myself away, listened to India Aire and waiting to exhale music while I vowed never to jump in the ring again. It didn't take long until I found myself suiting up and climbing right back into the ring, clenching my teeth preparing for the first punch. I had developed a habit in love that needed more than twelve steps. I needed a complete detox and fast! It still took a few more bruises and failed relationships to jump start what later became my saving grace. I forced myself to be honest and ventured deep into unchartered territory to find out "how" and "why" I felt stuck.

My Discovery

According to recent studies, over 44% of Americans are single (*United States Census Bureau 2013*). Records show there are approximately 40 million Americans who use online dating agencies and websites (*statisticbrain.com 2013*). Yet, according to a survey conducted by MSNBC, we are currently experiencing the highest rates of divorce and infidelity nationwide. While doing my research, I found that 88% of Americans between the ages of 25-32 believe there is a "soul mate" waiting for them. The U.S. census shows that within this same age group, divorce rates are higher and more cases of domestic violence have been reported. I found this information shocking with all of the latest in 12 steps to getting married, the best ways to keep your mate happy articles and blogs, love doctors, match makers and a plethora of finding love & self-help books. Being single made those statistics heart breaking and gave me a sense of hopelessness in ever finding my idea of "true love".

With the help of soap operas, reality television, sitcoms, music, movies and other popular media, it has become an addicting custom to investigate, spectate and commentate on unhealthy relationships drenched in flamboyant drama. As entertaining as it may be engaging in dramatic and unhealthy relationships has now become an epidemic in American Culture. Relationship drama has become so popular, that regardless of how educated or successful, men and women of diverse backgrounds have developed habits of embracing the drama in relationships and expecting unhealthy trends with mates and even friends. The trend has caught on so quickly that any image of a truly happy and healthy relationship is now interpreted as being an exaggerated fairy tale and mocked like botched art.

Thanks to what we have accepted, men and women alike enter into relationships suited up for battle; swiftly throwing punches at the first sounds of love. We enter into a tango of emotions; dancing around, sharing quick punches, cuts and bruises until both are too tired to put up anymore fight. It seems, as if, we wait until we have no fight left in us. We assume it's time to "settle down" and finally accept love or any available replica. We have adopted toxic rituals and habits in relationships, sharing beliefs such as "love is a game" and incorporating a language that instructs independence and disregard to feelings. Using phrases to describe our romantic interactions like "It is what it is" and breeding labels such as "Friends with

Benefits" portraying happiness while never experiencing it as truth.

Being all too familiar with the trends of love and drunken by the toxic habits in relationships, I used my own experiences and comparisons to the veterans of love, to identify and reconstruct a pathway to the answers that I've been in search of for countless years. I took drastic measures, interviewing my past rivals and reevaluating my filters through life only to discover that what I blamed the most for my unhappiness was the exact antidote I needed: LOVE. A word that started wars, and has brought success to media worth billions of dollars. I discovered that the same thing we're fighting against is what we're in need of the most and because of our filters in life, we have developed an immunity to it which makes us susceptible to unhealthy and most times toxics relationships.

Although statistics prove both men and women have equal amounts of heartaches, on average, it's the man who is perceived as the wolf and the woman who is the innocent sheep, unknowing of the dangers lurking about her. As a woman, it's easy for me to live as if I am unaware. The reality is, in love, men and women like to play "cat and mouse" teasing the curiosity of the Cheshire, dangling our little tails about, feeding off of the adrenaline of the chase only to kick and scream if we ever got caught--which is why we initiated the pursuit in the first place, right?

Although most men would disagree, women are craftier in the game of love. We find it most difficult to conquer with caution so, often times we find ourselves dangling in the ropes and locked away in the pockets of the ones we chose to challenge. Women were once celebrated but now have accepted being random trinkets stuffed in pockets of men only to be acknowledged for entertainment and traded for other objects of greater value. While it seems as if we are treated with cruel and unusual behaviors, the reality is women have found a sense of pride in settling for being the "main piece" and have divorced the thoughts of ever having long-term commitment and denying the true cries for security with a mate.

This book is designed to not only acknowledge the many ailments we share in love and relationships, but also to empower women to embrace their truths. My aim is to assist women in discovering their "how" and "why" and to ignite a passion that will lead them to their "who" and "when" in the quest for love. I have never claimed to have all of the answers nor, will I create a false hope that once her truth is found, life's relationships will become easier to manage. I simply aspire to prove that there is a way out of the cycle and recovery is possible. No matter how deep or far gone love may seem, the journey back to reality will unleash the power to accept what we deserve in life and in love as long as we make a conscious decision to stay out of the pocket.

Dedication

To my angels who smile over me: my Granny Mrs. Etta Mae Ford and my Dad Rev. Edward W. Alston.
Thank you for defining UNCONDITIONAL Love.

To my son Isaiah you are forever mommy's heartbeat.
You are my "why". Thank you for being the gift my life needed to succeed.

To the ladies of P.U.M.P.S. Women's Society, Inc.
Thank you for being my sisters and supporting me from the beginning. #PUMPS4Life!

Chapter 1:
"Truth Hurts"
The reality about relationships

From birth, we are conditioned to mirror an image of a certain role in society; little girls are dressed in cute pink outfits with bows and flowers while, little boys are costumed in little sailor suits, blue hats, and sports themes to induce a sense and understanding of feminine and masculine. Though gender roles are important in the psychological development of a child, it takes much more than pink and blue décor to stimulate the knowledge of one's own identity in gender. The same notion applies in relationships. No matter how many Disney 'happily ever after's' a person is exposed to as a child, it takes much more to mature the emotions necessary to engage and manage healthy relationships. Although, statistics prove a direct correlation between divorce rates and the probability of their children suffering divorce, it will be idiotic to believe simply exposing a child to a healthy relationship will guarantee success in their own. I'm reminded of parents who believe if they make their little boys play sports and tell them not to be too emotional or if they force their daughters to wear dresses and sit with their legs crossed as a 'proper lady' that magically it will repel them from homosexuality. Engagement and management of healthy relationships require not only exposure or examples, but also proper training and effective tools that are tangible to apply. While there is no mystic formula or script to promise you will experience a fairy tale type of romance, you can be assured that there is a map to help direct you through every choice you make in love.

There are countless books, articles, magazines, blogs and clinical essays about the challenges in love and relationships. Phenomenal research has been conducted to recognize new theories concerning the blend of personalities, culture, religion, and how these affect relationships and marriage in America. Only a few focus on ways to manage our encounters and even less give sensible explanation and/or tools to cure any disorders we have adopted in love. I strongly suggest, before entering into any type of relationship, you get a strong grasp of your personal positions in love. An amazing tool is a book that I use in many of my seminars: "The Five Love Languages," written by Gary D. Chapman. It gives a clear description of the 'languages' we embrace and is accompanied by a simplistic quiz that allows you to identify, what I like to call, your "Love Dialect". We can all agree that understanding our filters and how they affect our personal view is vital for successful relationship management. Understanding the differences in personalities between individuals and how they influence our perceptions is also important. At some point in our lives, we have come across what seemed to be the 'perfect' scenario that became the most painful and memorable lesson in love regardless of how much we understood the different viewpoints and filters.

I've always been curious about human behavior and our natural brain functions, curiosity was the only reason I chose to major in Psychology. After years of study, I found that we are not all created equal. The complexities we have in our mental and emotional process are present in our associations with love and relationships. Common psychological knowledge supports that we all have filters in life: our culture, nationality, religious beliefs, gender, age, and socioeconomic status all influence our reaction to challenges and our perceptions about success; the same applies in relationship management. For example, a Caucasian American female met the love of her life in college-an Asian American male. They met at a mixer, noticed they shared mutual friends and interests; they formed a friendship that would soon became love. After three years, into what she would describe as the perfect relationship, she began to inquire about meeting his parents. It was a bit unnerving that he had yet to invite her to meet his family and even more than that, he never showed an effort to meet hers. After consulting with her friends, she found that many of them met their boyfriend's family after an average of one year. This new census began to fuel fears, which encouraged her to pick, probe, and even initiate debates about how crucial it was for them to meet each other's family, especially, if he loved her as much as he claimed. After weeks of tiring arguments, he explained in his culture, introducing a love interest to the family was only done at the time of engagement and assured her that while his family knows about her and have seen pictures, he desired to complete his education before getting married. Once calmly discussed, she understood the severity of what seemed to be a simple gesture because of her constant pushing and aggressive behaviors; he now had doubts about continuing their relationship. The story ends with the two of them dating for only a year thereafter and ending as only friends. Being American means more than just citizenship; our country hosts hundreds of different languages and religions, it is a melting pot of ethnicities and cultures, which all effect our perceptions and experiences in dating, relationships, and love. Regardless of all the fables, parables, and fairy tales we have shared, the reality is, before we can begin a journey to gaining clarity about what we deserve in love, we must first understand there are extensive filters and variables that influence every individual in multifaceted ways. Once those philosophies are understood, we must then identify our own relation to them.

Women in Relationships

Since the beginning of time, women have had a bad rep when it comes to relationships. Throughout history, women have been the epitome of deceit, trickery, lies, and pure evil. It seems HIStory has placed us on the 'back burner'. It seems to be a common thread within various cultures to imprint a dark vision of women as a symbol of demise and death in love and relationships.

Regardless of the injustices we have been forced to endure, I must admit, we have played our part extremely well. Acknowledging the foundations of 'gender roles': men are the providers and women are the caretakers-we must take ownership of our own part in the paradigm shifting. Our aggressive nature and takeover attitude has locked us in a place we must revert from. By no means am I agreeing that women are inferior or should be subservient or to our male counterparts. I'm taking this opportunity to challenge traditions and introduce the thought: "What's wrong with being the 'best supporting actress' to the 'best leading man'? Contrary to popular distortions of feminism, if we never honor men as the leaders they were created to be, how could we expect them to stand as Kings? To take this thought one-step further, how can we expect these men to treat us as Queens? I am aware that by presenting this revolutionary thought, I have subjected myself to scrutiny. I challenge the naysayers, who will mainly be women, and pose this reflection: if what we're doing isn't working, when will we take a chance to try something different? Besides, 'repeating the same method and having expectations of a different outcome' is the definition of insanity. So, in theory, we're consciously agreeing with men that we as women are deliberately insane? (Selah)

Almost every woman has experienced a romantic relationship and those who have been hurt by love can attest to the fact that at some point she has entertained feelings of anger, bitterness, and some as drastic as rage. Yet, most will usually blame their extreme emotions on "him". Him-the one who once possessed your heart, was at one time the image of your 'forever' but has now been demoted to three lifeless letters that hold no value in description. Now, he has moved on and seems to feel nothing and you are left feeling like a used tissue, soaked in the worst of all he held inside. Women appear to be the ones left behind, while men move on like the number one draft pick-new team, new contract, and new benefits with the same game. Ladies, understand, men do have emotions and are able to communicate them honestly. We just need to recognize that their expressions are different from ours. Remember, we are not created equal. We were built with a variety of emotions in order to nurture a fully functioning being that requires all that we have to be all that they can. Men don't. They are basic: happy, sad, mad, sick, tired, hungry and horny. If a man is hungry, he will get something to eat. If a woman is hungry, she will calculate all of the variables: what she's in the mood for, who's going with her, what to wear, how far is it, what will it cost, what time of day, how many calories, and finally, what will be the aftermath of it all. By the time we've made a decision, the man has already finished his food, released in the bathroom, and is now horny and looking to you to satisfy him with physical dessert. Meanwhile, we're still focused on the food and feeling he's more interested in his sexual needs rather than our nutritional needs. Making a simple decision, like where to go for dinner, can create high emotions for women. We are intentionally created to use our emotions to nurture and bring life not to lash out and degrade. If we can learn how to choose our emotions, I will guarantee over half of our relationship issues will end. Because I know that will depend on the time of the month, the weather, how long we have in the relationship, the time of day, if it is around a holiday, or our birthday, I suggest we make the mature decision to learn how to manage our emotions.

The other part of our relationship challenges are more of a life practice:

discovering if we are either a thermometer or a thermostat. The thermometer is designed to gage the temperature surrounding it, while a thermostat is designed to alter the temperature surrounding it. Most women are thermometers. Partly because of poor emotional management, we allow whatever is surrounding us to change our temperament. If we walk in a room and no one acknowledges our new dress or hairstyle, we begin to second-guess our image, if we attend a wedding or baby shower; we get obsessed with our 'time clock'. No matter how high or low our temper, we depend on an outside stimulant to change it. Unfortunately, this responsibility is then impressed upon the men in our lives. In relationships and in life it best to make a choice to become a thermostat. This choice will lead to a method that is more proactive vs. reactive. A thermostat is motionless. It's mounted on a solid surface, and doesn't give an alert before making changes. Women, we can be most powerful when we take the time to gradually set our 'tempers' to positively influence our surroundings and relationships. When we recognize the power in making choices with calm and less erratic emotions, who knows what successes we can achieve in relationships and love.

For me, this lesson required daily reminders. I now have the wisdom to make decisions without regret, move forward in relationships, and love without hesitation. At the beginning of my journey, I believed my habits were a correct representation based on the person thought I was. I accepted what I believed I deserved until I found myself stuck in the darkest corner of the deepest pocket. In his pocket, trinkets, sticky wrappers, and feelings of being forgotten surrounded me; meanwhile, he changed his wardrobe and continued with life. It amazed me to learn how blind I was to the truth about my position in relationships and how many pockets I'd been in all in the name of "love".

I want to reiterate, having one in the pocket does not describe a cheater, although infidelity is quite possible. Based on the nature of the relationship, a pocket can be as deep and wide to hold all desires or small and tight without room for much at all. No matter the size of the pocket, it is always a destructive place to hold a heart.

Chapter 2: "Love Habits"

First thing in the morning, I like to have a hot cup of coffee. I'll admit that I enjoy coffee much more than average; I enjoy more than just the taste. The smell, the feel, and the experience invigorate me. It's become more than a habit, this is a custom I have started to begin my day. I will accept nothing smaller than a medium cup of coffee, flavored creamer, and a dollop of whipped cream. I prefer my coffee in the morning, but there are times a nice soothing cup on a cold evening, wrapped in a blanket, and soft jazz in the background is just what the doctor ordered. How I prepare my coffee is the same, I've done it so much that I guarantee I can do it with my eyes closed. No matter where I am, my body has become accustom to indulge in a blend of dark roast and sweet flavor as the sun rises and without it, chaos is a possibility. Coffee is my morning habit.

Regardless of what health enthusiasts advise me to be cautious of, it's a satisfying routine that I'm not willing to end.

In love, we establish the same addicting routines, rituals, and traditions that I've branded as our "Love Habits"©. Most of these habits exclude common sense; they are custom-made and unique to our approaches to relationships and love. Our love habits are influenced by a variety of stimulants: our culture, religion, family upbringing, and gender. These stimulants are also known as our "filters"- they create a sieve of which we use to decipher our preferences in relationships. Our love habits can began to evolve at an early age; if you grew up in a family where your father always worked and your mother stayed home, you can prefer to date or marry only men who make enough money that allows you to stay at home as your mother did. If you witnessed an unhealthy relationship between an interracial couple, you may prefer to date or marry only within your same race. Love habits are never created spontaneously they are first stimulated, nurtured, and then practiced until they become repeatedly implemented into your reactions to love. Many women will confuse their love habits as "standards". What kind of job he has, his physique, his hobbies and his talents are all desired based on your love habits. Standards are based on morals, values, character and ethics: his discipline, his work ethics, what he values, family, investments, etc. If you desire a husband who is nurturing, wants a family, and can keep a structured home, but you always seem to attract the "bad boy" you may be stuck in a habit of dating the opposite of what you truly desire. In love, your habits will almost never yield the results you need.

You can recognize your love habits by paying attention to the type of person you are. If you always seem to give to the men in your life: buy them gifts, loan money, or pay for his admission to an event regardless of the few times he has done this for you-please don't lie to yourself and label it as simply being a "giving person". The truth is: you've acquired a habit of giving to men who prove to not have same habits as you. Please don't interpret this as advice not to give but to take caution to the truth about the habits you've developed which brought you to your current position in relationships and love. Your truth could very well be that you are a giving person, but who you are should always reflect in the type of love you receive. If you are a giver, the balance in love will be to attract a giver/provider. You may have embraced habits you observed your mother or sister, some even attach themselves to habits based on what they've seen on television. Posing as an investigator in the relationship forces you to go through your man's wallet, hack his online accounts, or check his phone. These are all habits that taint the image of the real you. Some women create habits as protection from being mistreated, this will never cause them to understand why they can't achieve true love. The answer: you can only receive what's true in what you are true to. Love requires risk, but women have accepted a habit of believing "he" will arrive without effort or sacrifice. Although it may take a few experiences to learn, you can still be the person you are and detached from the habits you've practiced.

Just like it took years to cultivate these habits, it's going to take time to divorce them as well. There are love habits that women shared across generations. The most common is the "Time Clock"- the threatening sense of running out of time before you find true love. This habit is fueled by erratic emotions and fears of menopause. Most have found themselves caught in this habit at some point of their lives. The first signs will be: feeling anxious after four months of dating because he has yet to give you an official 'title' or feeling pressure to take the relationship to another level although he's not showing interest. Anxiousness is not your biological clock ticking, it's your reality slipping away. It is a fact that women do have a limited amount of time to have safer and more frequent pregnancies due to our constant loss of eggs, which leads to menopause. Understandably, women are fearful of the changes menopausal women experience: mood swings, hot flashes, and unwanted facial hair. Although menopause is a transition, women dread to see, it is an inevitable reality of aging and have nothing to do with your abilities of receiving the relationships you deserve nor finding true love.

According to medical research, the frontal lobe–the part of the brain that processes logic and reason is not fully developed until roughly age twenty-six in both women and men. This fact supports psychology's theories regarding our learning patterns: as a child, age 0-12, we learn by example-we do what we see; as an adolescent, ages 13-24 we learn by emotion. It is not until age 25 that we begin to learn by logic and use reason and apply critical thinking skills *(reference: www.npr.com Richard Knox article: "The Teen Brain: It's Not Grown Up Yet)*. These findings are directly linked to current statistics that show couples who are married before age twenty-five have a seventy percent chance of divorce while couples who marry after age thirty have only a thirty percent chance of ending in divorce *(National Center for Health Statistics)*. In order to maintain success in relationships and love we must use less emotion and more logic, which requires a fully matured frontal lobe. Therefore, the notion that we must hurry before time runs out should not be a factor if we are stimulated by our emotions. This is a habit that will set you up for failure. Think about how many relationships you've been in where you felt he was the right one, but it was never confirmed. Understand that with any theory there are exceptions to the rule.

As in many life situations, there are those unexplainable instances that come to shame all research, evidence, and statistics. These cases are so rare that living your life in hopes of being that "one in a million" will drive you to places you will need a miracle to escape from.

Love habits are common, everyone has them and there is no way of avoiding it. There is a way to ensure you cultivate the right habits vs. damaging habits. Your love habit can be as rewarding as a weekly workout routine or as deadly as a drug addiction. There are even some habits that can send you into obsessive-compulsive love disorder or "OCLD©". Women with OCLD are like a lose pit bull on a mail carrier, chasing after any whiff of love. These women are likely to pre-purchase their wedding gowns and reserve reception halls without the prospect of a ring or a fiancé for that matter. It is vital that you recognize which of your habits are healthy and which are potentially harmful. As you become conscious of your healthy love habits, you will be able to acknowledge the right reciprocation and enter into new relationships, in life and in love, with confidence.

The Cycle

I fell hard

And you just left me there

You saw me drowning in my own tears

And you walked away

You never took the time

You didn't throw a line

You left me behind

And in my mind

I'm thinking

"What the?!"

And from that moment on

I swore I would

Never do it again.

My phone rang

And as soon as I heard your voice

I knew what time it was

I played around with my words

Trying to make it seem like what it aint

What it wasn't

What it can't be

What it never was

What you never could

How I truly feel

And where you'll never be

But with only three words

You made me feel the need

To say sorry.

And from that moment on

I swore I would

Never do it again.

So this time

I made up in my mind

That I would leave all that BS behind

And cut all ties to anything

Linked to the old us

This time I was serious

No more drama

No more 'baby momma'

'cause you called me wifey

And I must admit

I get a 'lil highfey

With just the thought that

I might be

Only to be slapped with reality

That you still find it hard to take time

For me

I still refused to leave

'cause I remember the day

You cried for me

And from that moment on

I swore I would

Never do it again.

So here I am

With your son in my arms

And your daughter

Hand in hand

Looking up at the man

She'll never get a chance

To see

No happy daddy memories

Only examples of why

She'll never be the type of woman

To trust a man

She'll never truly understand

Her heart deserves a chance

She'll never feel she deserves true romance

From a man

'cause her heart still cries out

Remembering the day her daddy left her behind

Drowning in her own tears

The day you walked away

You never looked behind

Never threw her a line

And in her 'lil mind

He's thinking

"Daddy?!"

And from that moment on

She swears

She'll never do it again.

The cycle.

Will it ever end?

-Miz J

Chapter 3: "Pick Pockets"

Though I've had few intimate partners, I have experienced an assortment of men who've adorned me with their attention, gifted me with dates, and invigorated me with affirming words that kept me coming back for more, until they lost their flavor, becoming bland and withered in appeal. Like most singles, the process of dating intrigued me. How two people would find a common link and lock themselves into an intricate pattern of clumsy conversations, timid steps towards trust, and thoughtless expressions of attraction. This provides a massive dose of adrenaline that is pleasurably overwhelming. My dating experiences were a mixture of amazing and horrific. An assortment of men who knew all the right things to do and men who had an overabundance of inappropriate and offensive things to say. They presented their gifts with creativity and originality, all in the name of lust.

Like most, my dates began with a hook line: "You're not like any of the other women I've met." or "When will I have the pleasure of showing you a good time?" – The initial confirmation didn't take much effort. For me, it was like the previews during a movie: no matter what was thrown at me, he only had a few short moments to show the right things to get me interested in the full-length feature. I took pride in being "a cut above the rest" yet still baffled at the fact that no matter how good these men claimed I was, I never lasted long enough to be named in the ending credits. I trained myself to become a chameleon, adapting to the atmosphere he presented, to subliminally prove I was worthy of being his leading lady. Business men, street boys, old school thugs, divorcees, artsy rebels, shy guys, and even preachers all seemed to know exactly how to hook me. After making the rounds and the ritual of showing off their prized catch, they released me back into the stream with all of the other 'throw backs'.

At first, I did what most women do, I chose a physical feature to obsess over; devoted time and tithed into perfecting the imperfections I perceived to be the faults that made me insufficient. I lost weight, changed my hair, experimented with bold fashions, and even moved to a different neighborhood all to upgrade my image. Sure, my reasons presented as everything but the need for attention, while my subconscious and I made a pact to go into autopilot for any life crisis. There I was in my mid-twenties with no one to brag about on social media. I took the common route and bragged about all of the material things I had and labeled myself a "Boss". Being a proven boss gave me the status I loved. I had respect from men and women as someone who knew what she wanted in life, who worked hard to gain all she had, and who could get whatever she wanted. I wore that mask so well; I began to believe this was my true identity. My alter ego "the boss" was fearless and craved no man. She would only share her time as charity to any poor saint who was brave enough to subject himself to her emotional theatrics. I played this role well, until I encountered a few who seemed to have x-ray vision and threatened to expose the real me. I blamed everything but the truth. I told men they were too controlling, wanted to move too fast or they weren't someone I saw myself with for the long haul. Truthfully, I was trying to hide the fact that I afraid my cover would be blown. I was afraid these men would show my vulnerability and that I would end up right back fighting the cold dark waves of loneliness.

Like any ego gone rouge, I became aggressively paranoid, becoming a "sista soulja" slashing any shadows of vulnerability and painting myself an independent woman. Thanks to music by Destiny's Child, Mary J Blige, Keysha Cole and PINK, I had a personalized soundtrack, which became my mantra for surviving love and the men who tried to infect me with it. I convinced myself that I was in full control and that I would only share what I chose with those I deemed worthy. I was as organized as a professor and cultivated a system. If he had great conversation but was unattractive and lacked 'umph' I kept him as a phone buddy and rotated excuses of why exploring romance wouldn't work. Simple excuses like, "I've been hurt before" or "I'm too focused on my career for a serious relationship right now"; giving him just enough to keep entertaining me, but making sure not to feed into any fantasies. If he was attractive and gave me great conversation, but seemed to have the potential to hurt me, I remained available for him and made sacrifices, like staying on the phone until early morning on a weekday, yet kept quiet about my hopes and wishes for more. On the other hand, if he were an average guy, maybe a "church boy", I would remain in neutral just in case I needed someone to fall back on. I felt empowered by my system. I believed I was in control, but along the way, I encountered a few men who found a way to wiggle in a little too close and get me hooked.

Just like the majority of single women, my challenge was not finding a man who would date me or give me attention; my true challenge was finding a balance between what I wanted and what wanted me. I was caught in a habit of recycling men and feared entering uncharted territory. Because of my fear, I remained faithful to my system regardless, of its lack of success. Trying to escape the feelings of desperation, I made a few investments into the men I truly wanted to stay around. To some I assisted with homework or business ventures, I even loaned money knowing it wouldn't be repaid and to a few I gave myself physically. I would only invest in those that would show gratitude or a hint of thanks because I knew those would be the men who would come back for more. Recycling didn't seem dirty, because longevity and trust was being built along the way. If I had a solid routine with one, it helped to keep the others well managed. Out of the list of men who were incorporated in my system, there was only a hand full I recycled.

My recyclables were very special to me, they held a place somewhere in my heart that I fed and trained as memories of love. I gave them titles in private yet remained only they're "home girl" in public. Most would recognize this as "friends with benefits"- a relationship that requires very little commitment, has no definite title and is only fueled by pleasures. These types of relationships are always the most critical in a woman's life because these male friends of hers will be those one whom she relies on for affirmation and validation. These are the men who know how to get close enough to entice her to make sacrifices yet smart enough to remind her of the ego she claims is too busy for commitment of love. In these type of relationships, women are the most exposed and easily obtainable to be tucked away in the pocket.

Being in the pocket feels safe, you're always close enough to have association and will frequently be recognized as someone of value. The danger is that women who are in the pocket are often disregarded as someone who may be worthy of exclusive relations and are solely valued by their benefits alone. Reject the comfortable idea that having "friends with benefits" is the same as having "on the pocket" while there are similarities, the most critical differences are that the one in the pocket will never receive direct refunded benefits and are almost always hidden from the public eye. Being in the pocket gives an illusion of a committed relationship yet yields no promise. Depending on longevity and the benefits sacrificed, a woman can remain in the pocket for several years continuing to hold on to perceived fantasies, and running after the mirages of true love. While wearing my mask, my vision was blurred and I was oblivious to the reality of the habits, I set up for myself. I was unaware of how foolish I looked, parading around playing "big girl" unknowing of the pockets I was jumping in and out of. It would be easy for me to blame men for all they took, but in transparency, I know that I willingly gave pieces of me quickly, consciously, and disregarded my own self-worth. No matter which pocket I picked to climb in, I found satisfaction in being a trinket or a charm. Keeping my bad experiences on instant replay, I fueled my own fear of never being good enough to have what I was raised to believe I deserved. Consequently, I accepted my positions in the pockets of men. I covered up any spontaneous blemishes with lies of being in control and allowed my ego to feed false reports of success to my subconscious.

In the "Back Pocket"
The one who is always there.

During my dating daze, I encountered a few men who were just right. Too bad for them, I was looking for someone with a little something extra. If there was one who was too neutral, he didn't spark much interest. Living a good life with a steady job, nice clothes, decent home in a quiet neighborhood, a clean car that runs good on gas, with dreams to become better was all "blah blah blah" for me. I titled them "neutrals". I wanted the men who gave me a bit of drama; the ones who came from hard neighborhoods and jail yet managed to maintain; the ones who were greatly involved in church and the community yet lived an extravagant night life and held a sense of mystery, those were the ones who seemed to peak my interest. Truthfully, those ones fed my fears, insecurities, and validated my delusions. However, I always managed a way to hold on to the "neutrals". Whether it was just for conversation or to frequent coffee shops and discuss art, bits of the real me seemed to be fed by those moments and real friendships grew. Although some of the "neutrals" began serious relationships with other women, I still kept in contact. Since we never had any sexual exchanges, I was confident that I was no threat to their current relationships because having conversations, getting coffee, or a simple meet up was harmless despite the obvious attraction, we were just friends. My neutral friends could always depend on me. I was there if they needed someone to vent to during lovers quarrels; if they needed to get out of the house for some fun and no stress; if they wanted a female's perspective on a relationship challenge; needed a few bucks for gas until payday or just couldn't sleep and needed late night entertainment. My friendships with "neutrals" were stress free and didn't require much attention. The fact that they all were getting serious with other women made it easier for me to be free to roam with complete openness and honesty. I could share my experiences with men and receive the same amenities I offered them during their challenges. Most would think these types of relationships are harmless yet this belief demonstrates the common disregard to the truth and will settle a woman in the 'Back Pocket'.

Women find themselves in the back pocket in most relationships. It's the easiest to access on a man and has the most room to maneuver around which makes it the most comfortable. I was most comfortable with Brian. I met him through a mutual friend; she and Brian met at Underground Atlanta where he worked and she liked to shop. In the beginning, Brain was just a name but after frequent interactions, she shared with me how much he intrigued her and that she was interested in getting to know him on a deeper level. My friend, was not much of a dater, she grew up in a sheltered home, so when she admitted to her attraction we all knew this guy was something serious. Like most girls in college, she depended on her friends to be her sounding board, talking about the times she took the train for nearly an hour and a bus just to have a quick peek at Brain while he worked. Her excitement grew as she discovered more details about his friends, where he lived and his hobbies. After a few months, she came to a couple of us and pleaded that we accompany her to a party that Brian was hosting at his house. She tempted us with the descriptions of his roommate and friends so we were on board without much pressure. We get to meet cute new men, party and she gains an outlet to get closer to her new love interest; it was a win-win situation. Once we arrived at Brian's house, we were pleasantly surprised to be the only women in attendance. A house full of tall, handsome, athletic men and we only needed to split it three ways. We made a pack that Brian was hands off and established a plan of attack and retreat in case things go sour. To our delight, the men were perfect gentlemen in their own rights, with a mix of humor, talent, and muscles beyond our wishes. Brian was the type of man who seemed to have no enemies. He was hospitable; made sure we had enough to eat and kept our cups filled. He even made sure to slip a warning to stay clear of the men he knew where looking to trap one of us in the back room. After hours of great fun, Brian made sure we left the party together and arrived home safely; he even called each of us to confirm we were secure. I was a bit surprised after getting my phone call from Brian to tell me how much he appreciated us coming and invited us all back a few weekends later for an instant replay. I had to make sure to share my delights and that night Brian and I talked on the phone for over an hour. We shared jokes and stories, found out we had the same interests…now let me pause to kill what I know you're probably thinking: the answer is NO- Brian and I never went out on a date nor did he make any advances towards me. I honored my rule of never getting involved with one of my friend's love interest. Brian and I did keep our conversations a secret for a while, for the obvious reasons of not wanting any false accusations or rumors to start. Our conversations always started out random and ended with him expressing how he truly felt about my friend and asking my opinion. Unfortunately, the feelings that she had weren't mutual, but I still refused to take the opportunity. Brian and I acknowledged a mutual attraction but agreed to remain friends. We went to dinner, he took me to games, and I helped him with business plans, homework, and even helped him find a second job. Our friendship grew and lasted beyond the failing relationship he and my friend had. After about a year, Brian began dating another woman but we never lost contact. He came to my job at Victoria's Secret to find nice gifts for her that I assisted him in choosing, and I received the sales credit. It became habit for Brian to come to me for whatever he needed regarding a relationship and I was blind to see that I had become his "go to girl" for satisfaction. It didn't bother me at first because we were 'just friends'.

It wasn't until his break up that it was made clear what my position was with Brian. He and his girlfriend were arguing about me; she expressed her discomfort with how close I was to Brian and how she found it difficult to believe, he and I had never entertained any sexual curiosities. When he brought it to my attention, I laughed and mocked her, claiming she was jealous because she couldn't be as close to him as I was. I explained how "things happen for a reason" and that it was best for them not to be together because he deserved someone who understood him completely and wasn't as controlling. I deemed her immature and found humor in the fact that I caused her to feel secondary. He was hurt and mourning his lost yet I felt a sense of power, just knowing I affected that much of his life that he would come to me after losing the woman he obviously loved. Here I was smiling while someone I claimed to care for was in pain yet distracted from his feelings because of my own selfishness. Truthfully, I was relieved his relationship ended, that way I can have my 'friend' all to myself.

Women in the back pocket, survive off DENIAL-identified in psychology as one of the best-known defense mechanisms. While in the pocket, it's the easiest way to nurture your ego, protecting it from the truths we can't cope with. The truth is I hid from the facts-I was attracted to Brian. I had convinced myself that being his friend was the next best thing. Truthfully speaking, the only reason why I didn't make advances towards him was because I feared being the same position of rejection as my friend; losing to vulnerability. My ego allowed me to falsify a relationship between the two of us and justify how unorthodox it was in reality. All that I invested in Brian was to be compensated with, attention and affirmation. My own insecurities made it easy for me to make myself available to him regardless of what I was not receiving in return. My habit was to accept what I believed I deserved based on what I perceived I wasn't worthy of. Therefore, I became a resident of Brian's back pocket.

Becoming a resident of the Back Pocket is simple; it only takes a potential relationship with a man and denial. Most find this a challenge to accept, mainly because once we're introduced to reality, we are quickly bombarded with flashes of how many back pockets we've been in and out of and, for some, are currently stuck in. Therefore, we then revert to what is comfortable: we deny it. Although the back pocket is the most common place for a woman to be with a man, it is also the easiest to get out of. Remaining in a position for a man to reach back to you to accommodate his needs without him committing to give them in return is choice you make while in denial. If I would have accepted the truth about Brian from the beginning that he entertained his curiosity about me and enjoyed my company yet was never interested in having a serious relationship with me; my approach and reactions to him would have been much different.

Therefore, the remedy is to accept the truth about your relationship with him. Yes, freedom from the back pocket is as simple as accepting the truth. If accepting the truth were truly an effortless task, you wouldn't be in denial in the first place, right?

In the "Jacket Pocket"
Neither Hot or Cold .

Moving back to California after twelve years was a leap of faith for me. Everything I became, the wisdom I've earned was mass produced in Georgia and leaving it all behind was one of the most frightening choice I had to make. I jumped around a few cities before settling back in my hometown, while still hanging on to the possibilities of retreating back to Georgia. One of the main factors that encouraged me to stay was working as assistant to my brother during his process of completing his first solo album project. Having that bond and working in my passions with a fresh outlook, in new territories was intriguing and satisfying. As his assistant, I was able to do what I loved without the pressures and demands that I was once consumed with. It was invigorating to experience his process and witness the benefits of his creative metamorphosis.

Interacting with a variety of creative minds satisfied my craving for spontaneity.

While auditioning for a new band, it was my responsibility to conduct the initial screening and correspondence with all of the musicians. Because of my years of administrative proficiency, I became very mechanical during this process; incoming and outgoing emails, phone interviews and appointment scheduling didn't take much energy nor did it require much thought. I easily operated in autopilot... until there was a breach in the system.

His name was Terrell-a young percussionist living in Los Angeles. I didn't know much about him outside of his performance resume and contact information. Nothing about him interested me except for; he had the skills necessary to complete the project so, I scheduled a phone interview. I started the screening process much like I had the many times before: swift and direct questioning, emotionless responses but he frequently took me off course by asking probing questions and injecting his quick wit and sarcastic humor while using a comforting and familiar tone. I remained professional and asked every question required and successfully scheduled his audition but made the mistake of complimenting him on his interview, which lead to a conversation that lasted nearly two hours. We discussed everything from our favorite genres of music, debated about the best fast food meals to have after midnight and even shared a common love for a properly prepared plate of Chicken Alfredo. Although we had yet to see each other in person, I was already hooked.

My brother and I established a "spill proof" system that left nearly zero room for error. With my great administrative insight and his keen ear for talent, only the elite in ability could infiltrate our establishment and Terrell did. Despite the flamboyant conversations prior to his auditions; he had the talent, the experience, and was available which was exactly what we needed for the project and was exactly what the doctor ordered for a brewing personal 'project' of my own. I made sure never to interfere with business so I made a silent vow not to contact him again until instructed for professional purposes only. It took weeks, but as soon as I was giving the green light, I called with a smile and without restraint, I allowed him to dance with my mind to the tunes of our creative passion harmonies. It didn't matter that he was over five years younger than me, or that until this point we'd only saw pictures of each other on social media. I didn't even factor in what his relationship status might be. Thoughts of if he were interested in anything romantic with me never crossed my mind. I was convinced I didn't need any of that. Curiosity was the culprit and its satisfaction was my only motive.

Weeks transformed into months and Terrell and I were locked into a beautiful conversation tango. He called at the right time, every time, regardless of my obligations and knew just how to lead with the perfect combination of precise topics and technical flirtation. Mutual attraction was confessed but we both held on tight to the simple promise of 'something deeper' to avoid a sloppy experience that would inevitably end in tears and anger. We shared intimate matters: past heartbreaks and current heartthrobs even escorted one another on a spiritual journey through our beliefs and faiths. He was defined as a true friend, proving his rank with every genuine compliment. After months of phones calls, shared photos, and Skype adventures, we agreed finally to meet in person; we had no romantic expectations and was secure in our abilities to enjoy shared company yet refused to ignore the possibilities.

It had been nearly a year and a few failed attempts to meet between his gigs and tours that I finally got a chance to meet up with Terrell during my holiday vacation with family in southern California. I endured a ten-hour drive, three of which were due to my mother's confidence in the wrong route around the mountains, with my four year old son and my uncle's frequent need for potty breaks just to get a quick taste of freedom, to let my hair down and enjoy whatever developed in the City of Angels. After days of preparing what would be the biggest new year's gumbo feast ever, we finally arrived at my cousin's house in West Los Angeles, I loved her retro home that was passed down to her from my aunt and although she added some contemporary upgrades, it still held the frames of many great childhood memories. Because her two bedroom one bath home was filled with over seventy people, I thought it was the perfect opportunity to finally meet Terrell face-to-face without the awkwardness of being in a forced romantic setting. That way, if any 'catfish' scenarios appeared, family would already be safely surround me.

I tried to be nonchalant about inviting him over for gumbo but the truth was I was excited about putting a body to the voice that had comforted me and intrigued me for so long. I can remember checking my lip-gloss about five times before he arrived, and even trying to change my shoes but he drove up right in the middle of me searching the car for a more relaxed ensemble. It was dark out but the street light illuminated his smile and before he took a step out of the car, I was already mesmerized. He didn't hesitate to hug me, one of those hugs that epitomized the essence of 'warm embrace'. With his firm arms around me, I was able to get a whiff of his cologne that made me close my eyes while pressed against his chess. This moment was not rushed, he took his time and in that moment, he said all I thought he would without words. We did a lot of smiling yet it wasn't awkward at all, it felt as if we'd known each other for years. Unfortunately, the moment was short lived due to my mother's urge to return to the hotel to sleep, so with a quick goodbye we agreed to meet up that weekend after my brother's live performance. As I watched him drive away, my thoughts began to wonder: is he really THIS good? Why does he have to be younger than me? Am I crazy? If he IS all that he seems, how long will I be able to indulge? Before I could begin to find answers to any of these questions, he sent a simple text: "You're beautiful." … it was right then and there that I knew, he was going to be the kind of trouble I would be happy to get into.

It was Wednesday and the weekend couldn't come quick enough. I was excited to see my brother perform and I wanted to have a night to myself in a lavish hotel and do whatever I wanted. We all know I was also anxious to see Terrell again. I booked a room at the fanciest hotel I could get to and took my time to prepare for my brother's show that night. I threw all inhibitions out the window, had a glass of wine while I took a bubble bath and waited for the car my brother sent to deliver me to the venue in NOHO. I wanted to dance with anyone and everyone who was brave enough. I invited Terrell to join us, but unfortunately, he was at a gig but promised to return to me after. The night was amazing, filled with music, drinks, and laughs. After an amazing show, my brother and a few friends went for a late night snack and they took me back to my hotel where I met up with Terrell. I couldn't tell if it was the mix of martinis or if I truly knew what I was getting into but I felt relaxed. I don't remember much of the walk up to the room but once we entered, all doubts, fears, and battles with reason and logic left me. It was the very first time we were alone together but it felt like we were right where we belonged.

After a few laughs and clumsy moments in the dark, Terrell and I were sucked in into a vacuum of passion and shared one of the most exhilarating moments I have ever experienced. In that one night he proved that age truly is only a number, and although we didn't talk about much, so much was spoken without words. I remember feeling unguarded and vulnerable; he made it easy and as the morning approached, he kissed me softly on the forehead and left me cradled between oversized pillows and feeling beautiful.

While this rendezvous seems like the beginning of a romantic novel, it was the beginning of the most emotionally confusing experiences I've ever had in relationships. Like most women, I was swept away by the fact that Terrell was able to speak to me in a way no other man had before. I was sold on his conversation, his good looks, his talent, and sense of humor yet the one thing I failed to take into account was his availability. Terrell gave me the attention I wanted, yet he wasn't too pushy for time. He was confident and open to share the truth about what he felt and seemed to be perfect, but it all made me fall apart. As women, we make it a habit to outline everything that we desire in a mate. We construct a list of requirements, qualifications, standards and amenities. We will often find ourselves praying that we meet the man who has it all and he falls madly in love with us. Often, once we meet the man who has it all, or even seventy percent of what we've been waiting for, we revert to an attack mode and try to discredit everything he's presented on our wish list. It has always puzzled me how much we ask for then as soon as we get it, we label it as a lie because we truly don't believe we deserve it. Terrell never pushed me into anything, never made strong advances to commit to a serious relationship but because of the love habits I was committed to, my emotions reacted to what my mind told me I deserved, which was the opposite of what my spirit and my heart knew as truth.

After an amazing crescendo of shared emotional and passionate expressions with Terrell, my mind went into attack mode without any logical strategy. I began to be more aggressive and sarcastic. I tested everything he had already proven to be sincere. I played "I'm not feeling him as much as he thinks I am… although I know he knows how much I really am" games and laughed at any sign of exposed truth. He started calling less; speaking every other day to maybe once or twice every other week. It soon became rare that I would hear from him at all so I did what most women do when our "card is pulled" -I bluffed and landed myself in an emotional tug of war between what I want, what was right in front of me, and what I believe I deserved. Although he took his time, never pressed, or tried to manipulate me in any one direction, I wrapped myself in every frantic, delusional emotion, and hid behind every excuse to avoid vulnerability, which made him feel confused and caused him to back up in defense. He gave me the space he felt was needed and it was then that I realized how much I truly needed to be honest; not just with him but with myself. It took months, but once I was completely honest and was freed of the perception fears I entertained I became more receptive to what I truly wanted from Terrell and that was all he had given. Understandably, it took him a while to reopen the doors but once he did, our friendship seemed better than how it began. However, not without me having to swallow my pride and apologize with every ounce of honesty I held inside. It was the most exposed I had ever felt.

The challenge about being in the jacket pocket is not the other person, it's your reactions to the relationship and the only vehicle for escape is honesty. This is one of the few positions where the one in the pocket has the most control. While in the jacket pocket, you feel as if you are a perfect fit: supplying the needs of your mate and feeling secure in potential for long-term affection yet your emotional reactions and lack of openness can land you hung up until the season changes again.

Finding yourself in the pocket can be hurtful. At times, it brings a sense of worthlessness like every piece of lent, soiled tissue, and crumpled bits of unwanted paper. It can get lonely and leave you feeling like a forgotten washed dollar, limp, and lifeless. Although it's a harsh reality, your position in the pocket is not always a result of your actions alone. There are times when you will be placed in the pocket for only a moment then taken out before you even notice. Most women who experience this yo-yo effect in relationships are in the Jacket Pocket. Being in the jacket pocket can be confusing yet it's the most easiest to expose. There are a few simple tools that will allow you to avoid this constricted position, yet the challenge is that the responsibility is all on YOU.

In the "Front Pocket"

Almost does not count.

College was the greatest and the most difficult time of my life. Attending the top HBCU in the nation for women brought pressures from all sides of the earth that I don't believe I was prepared for. Being a "Spelman Woman" meant more than affiliation by definition, wearing that mantel did yield many benefits. In my second year in college, I was living in a three bedroom, two bath home and assistant manager at one of the most popular lingerie retail stores in one of the hottest cities in the nation. Young, educated, and ready to take on the world. Most circumstances, like finding out my first love cheated on me, didn't affect me as deeply as it may have other women with less going for them. A selfish boastful fact that helped me get over the heartache yet was furthest from the truth.

I slipped into a functional depression, smiling and having an amazing time with friends but fearful of being alone with my own thoughts of why I wasn't good enough. I kept myself busy with extra hours at work, girls' night out every weekend and spontaneous dates with men I had no interest in all to avoid confronting the truth replaying in my thoughts. I was throwing away money on material things I never needed and burning my friends out on too many parties. It was mid-terms and the fall was settling in. I would cringe at the sight of lovers cuddling on park benches watching the leaves fall. I saw each orange, yellow, red, and brown leave as a tear that I was fighting to keep from falling. So, I continued with making new friends who were just as financially careless as I was to distract my heart.

I got an invite to join a few 'friends' to a house party clear across town. None of my girls wanted to spend another night with loud music and annoying men so I decided to go solo hoping I could manage to keep myself entertained around a house full of tipsy college guys without looking like a bone to pass around. After over an hour train ride, I was instructed to call for my ride from the metro station. All dressed up on public transportation is like setting a disabled zebra in a lion's den. I got old drunks and homeless men proposing to me and the further out the train went, it seemed the worst the company became. I had almost had enough and contemplated returning home until a man came and sat in the seat facing directly in front on me. He gave a quick smile in acknowledgment; it soon became awkward trying to avoid frequent eye contact since he was the only one in my field of view. After a few uncomfortable glances out of the blurred window, he got up and sat right next to me. My first reaction was to jump off at the next stop but he cordially introduced himself and escorted me into a conversation that seemed to take my mind off the forty-five minute train ride I still had ahead.

Kendrick was dripping in confidence and spoke in a king's tone. He had a thick country accent that leaked hits of southern charm. He poked around to find out what I was getting myself into and invited himself to chaperon while I waited for my ride. It was a relief he was there and a sad reality check when the guys who planned to pick me up never showed. I was embarrassed to confess that I had wasted two hours of travel time for a party filled with men I barely knew, so I stumbled to find an explanation of why I was turning around. Kendrick called my bluff quick and advised I allow him to accompany me back to my destination since it was late and being alone on public transportation at that hour wouldn't be wise. I didn't know if it was a blessing or a set up but I was relieved and accepted. The train ride back seemed to last only a few short moments as Kendrick and I laughed, flirted, and shared our whole life story with each other . I asked his purpose on the train and he answered, "To meet you". Kendrick then became my reason to smile again.

After exchanging numbers and being guided safely home, Kendrick and I became close as quickly as we met. He knew all the right things to say and all the best things to do in all the right ways. He would give me rides home from work when it rained and gave me company at the grocery store, and as a thank you, I'd cook for him. Thank God for a southern grandmother, because I believe my great cooking skills kept him coming back when I had nothing else to offer, but it wasn't long before I shared with him all I had to offer. Being in a relationship with a southern man was something new to me. I had to learn quickly how to please without words and stay supportive without advice. Kendrick made that easy for me. Even after a few immature 'hiccups', he remained faithful. Kendrick was always open to talking things out which was foreign to me. He never raised his voice regardless of how upset he was he made sure to tell me he loved me before bed. Having a man as confident as Kendrick who was willing to be open and vulnerable with me made it easy for me to surrender and submit to whatever he needed me to be. I found myself making sacrifices for him unlike any man I had cared for in the past. I even introduced him to my mom and embraced his family as my own. For me, Kendrick was more than enough and I began to move forward in life with plans of being by Kendrick's side accented with his last name. We openly discussed our future together and he frequently assured me that his plans were to keep me right where I was. I wasn't aware at the moment but those conversations were the threads securing me in his front pocket.

Kendrick had everything I wanted but was far from perfect. Despite his past, I accepted him and all that came with it. His family embraced me and supported us, which gave me a sense of security. We didn't officially live together but needless to say, he was free to stay with me as long as he desired. Soon the walk-in closet was split into 'his and hers' and my one bedroom apartment became home for the love we were building. Our relationship felt natural. He did all he could to bring home the bacon and I made sure to keep the house clean and fried it up. I took pride in fulfilling domestic duties to benefit our home. I was free to love him and he did everything I loved to prove how dedicated he was to "us". Like most relationships, ours came with a few challenges. After the first year, Kendrick and I had experienced nearly every storm a relationship could withstand. From temporary break ups to family crisis, although it got shaky, we always found our way back in the safety of each other.

Fresh out of college, living in midtown Atlanta, Ga. I made up in my mind; I knew exactly what I wanted and who I wanted to be with me. Kendrick was my perfect fit.

Understanding I had felt that way about a few men before, there was none that stayed like he did nor were they willing to sacrifice as much as he was. His dedication to our relationship was all the proof I needed to be devoted until the end. He gave me more than I had ever received from a man and reassured me that I was the type he wanted to build a future with and that was the bait that allowed me to willingly inhabit Kendrick's front pocket.

For most women, the front pocket seems to be the best place. It's the most challenging to occupy because it's the closest to everything that a man deems valuable so women find it rewarding to be in such a place. The front pocket is the type of relationship that shows the most potential but the harsh reality is the potential is not promise. While it may seem to be the best place to be, the longer you remain in the front pocket the more damaging it is to be ripped out. Many front pocket relationships have led to a long-term commitment but also features the highest rates of infidelity and divorce. The challenge of being in the front pocket is knowing when to get out which is much more crucial than the time spent in any other pocket. Many women remain in the front pocket for well past five and sometimes even ten years before they begin to realize that no true commitment is coming. It's the couple that's lived together for years, some even have children yet he never finds the "right time" to propose. Most men, who have their mate in the front pocket are masters at 'reasons of why not'; money, waiting for children (if you haven't conceived any already), work/business, education, and aspirations to relocate will always be the foundation of their arguments. Why should you continue to give your all while receiving their 'whatever they choose to offer'. It is at these moments when women find it hard to decipher the reality of the bigger possibilities that he isn't "the one". It is a constant struggle between what you know you deserve and what you're afraid to let go of. While in the front pocket, you are the closest to his valuables. You may have access to his money, may share a house, bills, car, may have close relationships with his family or even have children with him, but if he believes that a full legal commitment, is not worth it, then you're locked in his front pocket and it is there you'll face the reality of your worth.

In the "Pocketbook"
For valuables only.

Throughout history, our definitions of masculine and feminine have traditionally remained the same: to be identified as masculine is to possess qualities or characteristics similar to a man: strong, aggressive, and powerful. Traditionally to be feminine relates to all things woman: daintiness, to be gentle, graceful, and soft we forbid the two ever become crossed. Yet, in love, most of us are hermaphrodites at heart. We all, men and women, contain the ability to have both feminine and masculine characteristics in love. There are men who are softer at heart and who are gentle in love but are regarded as weak and seem to be labeled as a "good guy" who will never finish first. It seems women complain about the things desired but are attracted to the men who openly deny us of those very requests. We have become schizophrenic in relationships; wanting what we don't have and accepting what we don't need while hoping he's morphed into what we perceived to be what we deserve. We want the man who looks like Tyson Beckford, who can be as romantic as James Garner, as humorous and wise as Steve Harvey, yet as dangerous as Vin Diesel? If such a man ever existed, he'd be emotionally unstable, controlling and jealous, hot tempered, verbally abusive and too damaged by his past to be able to securely manage a relationship. We have been swept away by fantasy, and while I do believe we need to insure our standards are secure-we must be clear about our personal reality and not one created by movies, music, fashion or word of mouth.

Because our goals are to mimic what we perceive in love, we have adopted characteristics that oppose what we claim as value. We are trained to be "ladies": soft, gentle, delicate and pretty but most of us are the complete opposite at heart. We fight over men, are argumentative, harsh with our words, manipulative, and downright ugly emotionally in love. We have made so many unfavorable choices that we're too damaged to notice that the men we attract are responding to the truth about our hearts. If you're the type of woman, like I was, who seems to always attract the type of man who doesn't want long-term commitment, or if you continuously find yourself being the 'other woman'. There's a part of you that's speaking louder than any other is, as mine did, screaming you truly don't believe you're ready or deserve all you claim. Most women in this position find it easy to become more masculine: more controlling, aggressive, and rigid. These women have been hurt by their choices so often that they struggle with trust. They have developed a habit of blaming their issues on the lack of trust in men but labor with trusting themselves even more. They believe being in control is the best way to protect themselves from repeating the past hurts and put themselves in masculine roles placing most men in their POCKETBOOK.

Women who carry men in their pocketbook *(the southern term for purse)* are the most hurt by their experiences in relationships and love. Most of these women are single mothers, divorcees, or come from extreme examples of both, in worse cases have been abused, which opens the door for a wide variety of entangled pockets that require much deeper therapy to achieve complete healing, which is very possible. A pocketbook, for a woman is equivalent to a man's wallet and/or front pocket; it's where we hold the things we deem most valuable. Our pocketbook, no matter how great or miniscule, can carry a lifetime of memories, fears, dreams, and aspirations that are resilient enough to shape or reshape the course of any relationship for the negative or positive. Unfortunately, most inhabitants of the pocketbook are doomed.

It's not easy for a man to reach the pocketbook. Sadly, it takes all the right things with the wrong woman or the wrong things with the right woman to be zipped up. Most men, who are genuine, honest, upfront, and carefree about their affection, will more than likely find themselves in the pocketbook. These woman are so accustom to the opposite that they automatically believe that one day the man will prove what she's believed for so long-that she can't get a man to actually give her what she desires, so she'll place him in the pocketbook. This position can be most draining to the men caught in it because like a fly caught in a spider's web, she'll drain him of all he has until he is lifeless in love. He can start as the nice man who always assists her with her groceries to the car, or the mature man who fixes her car. He can began as the flirtatious colleague, the polite guy at the gym, or even the understanding minister. Regardless of how he begins, if he's not careful, he can end up the 'good guy gone bad'.

Most women who trap men in their pocketbook feel damaged and get a sense of satisfaction from their posed revenge on 'the ones who hurt her'. She is seductive and manipulative, often using what the man wants to lure him. These women are extremely clever yet don't recognize their actions as negative. They believe that they have reached the end of their hope in love and find that keeping a man in their pocketbook is the final option. Sadly, most of these women have given up on love, but find it difficult to be alone, and fail to see merit in being single. These women keep a man to fulfill a particular need and/or have a few men to maintain a sense of value.

There were times in my life, especially after a breakup, that I felt the need to have a man in my pocketbook. I would label him my 'best friend', my 'brother' or even pantomime being in a relationship to keep him coming back. The men in my pocket were the ones who knew how to compliment me and who validated what I couldn't believe about myself. They were men who initially avoided romance, but found common interests and were willing to invest in me. Some would invest money, there were men who could fix things around my house, free admission to special events, and even sexual profits. Like most women in my position, after a breakup a felt belittled and inferior; having these men in my pocketbook gave me a sense of power and allowed me to be who I thought I should've been. Many who carry around an emotional pocketbook are haunted by memories of their failed relationships and use men like bandages to temporarily fix the hurt they entertain. Unknowingly, the men feel pride in providing a 'relief' yet will find themselves tangled in a web of emotional outbursts or left behind feeling unfulfilled which leads to his choice of finding another. And so begins his attempts for escape leading down a vicious path.

The pocketbook is complicated and filled with emotional compartments that men will never completely understand. It will begin as a simple flirtation with a woman who seems to have 'a good head on her shoulders' and progress as a mature agreement. What most men fail to recognize is exactly where they've been placed in the pocketbook: an inside zipper; an open compartment; or deep at the bottom lost among all of the leaking makeup, note paper, receipts and forgotten trinkets that lost luster somewhere along the way. The difference between men and women in the pocket is once a man has recognized where his place is, he will more than likely attempt to escape without a need for explanation or debate. Women, have a deeper need for communication that entrap them in emotions. Having a man in the pocketbook takes organization, superb management and logic, which will never work with emotions:

something us women have yet to learn how to control. We believe if things are going the way we want them, at the moment, we want it, progressing at the rate we desire with planned spontaneity, then we've achieved perfection in love.

The pocketbook is a symbol of what women believe they need to control. Hosting hidden compartments, a combination of flaps, zippers, buttons and faux adornments; men become victims of unstable, unpredictable, emotional outburst that degrade his perceptions of a 'real woman' and dilute his desires to settle in any serious romantic commitment. Although the pocketbook may be a complimenting accessory, it's filled with almost everything we never need, weighs us down, and works as the best place to transform any man with good intentions into a cold, defensive, and angry form of what we use to love.

Chapter 4:

"Pocket Detox"

Before anyone can make a choice to 'fix' or change anything about his or herself or the lives around him or her, they must first acknowledge the truth about having a problem. For women, it's become popular practice to label the problem 'Him". Thanks to a wave of 'independent women' mass media, we've adopted the notion that we can be much better without a man, yet we pattern our fashion, physique, personalities, and our lives for the attention of men. Whether we're trying to prove we're better by ourselves or the best before they entered our lives, we are conditioned to believe that 'they' are the enemy and we need to somehow conquer them only to win power and control? The sad truth is that we're fighting against something we have no clear understanding of and striving for something we've never seen. So before we can begin our journey to become greater, we need a complete DETOX-a cleanse from all of the old thoughts, perceptions and habits we've adopted which requires the one thing we claim to be a major challenge: commitment.

There are many people who maintain they are 'afraid' of commitment, mainly men. For most women in the pocket, we have adopted this common statement as truth. There have even been books, articles, and talk shows supporting the notion that there are people who have some sort of condition. This feeling imprisons them in a fear so profound that the mere thought of committing to someone long-term will send them into uncontrollable acts that are detriment to the wellbeing of their relationships. We talk about it and some have even admitted to falling ill with the same symptoms when we couldn't be further from truth. The fact is if he can work, attend parties, attend church, run a business, or even move in with a woman for over a year he has no problems with commitment: the ability to be dedicated to a cause, action, etc. He's been committed to his job, his friends, his money, his car, even coming home to you while you've been committed to maintaining a home. He's completely capable of the action of commitment. The challenge he has is engaging in that action towards you. In order to properly detox, we must first admit: we have been taught falsely and we need to break free from those habits and unlock the truth about what we deserve in relationships and in love.

Relationships and love have always been referred to as a 'game' or 'the chase'. In this state, we have been trained to accept that it is the man's job to hunt and chase until he has captured what he's after and women must remain frail, innocent, and vulnerable. We should then give in to whatever he demands to ensure pure happiness and peace despite being exposed to centuries of examples of this relationship model failing miserably. Women who claimed to be in the game always become confused about when to begin the chase, when to surrender, who should have the power, and who to blame if none of it works. Many have even been successful in getting 'caught' finding someone to join as life partners. Still, most will admit that once signed on the dotted line, their lives together became something mutated from what they once believed. It is now, that we must sieve through the truths about what works, what will not, and what we want.

My main challenges in my past relationships were quite simple: I first wasn't clear on what I deserved, which allowed me to willingly be chased by someone without being clear about what he wanted. The truth was that after each failed attempted I hadn't taken the time to heal. Being in the pocket is not the challenge, even escaping from the pockets of men don't take as much effort as it does to maintain freedom from the pockets. If you continuously run through relationships without proper healing and alone time to establish yourself as whole, you will be tossed around through pockets feeling like a used tissue.

Understand, breaking a habit that took years to develop is not going to disappear in a few weeks, not even months and for some of us it may take years before we're completely healed. Just like a drug, your love habits have become a part of your daily lives and you'd be lying to yourself if you believe that all will be different by the completion of this book. This process will require sacrifice, pure honesty, time, and most important patience.

The number one new year's resolution for women in America is weight loss. Each year the health and fitness industry will earn billions of dollars from new gym memberships, vitamins, juicers, and workout apparel. Most women have all the right intentions to become healthier for various reasons that are significant to their lifestyles. It's a proven fact that over half of the women who begin dedicated, lose hope, give up, and compromise their resolution to a more relaxed and substandard solution. The struggle that women share is not their desire, drive, or their abilities; it is setting an unrealistic goal and astronomical expectations. Beginning as a two hundred fifty pound woman at a size twenty-four and expecting to transform into a one hundred fifty pound woman who wears a size nine in a mere three months is impossible according to the best, health savvy standards. The same applies in love. To make a decision to have healthier and more positive experiences in love and relationships is a great goal. To believe that you will be able to find true love and a life partner within a matter of months after years of accepting and practicing the complete opposite will only set you up for a relapse. This could send you into a spiral of unhealthy habits that will hurt you even deeper than before. The best method is to take realistic steps towards practicing healthier relationships one experience at a time. Create a love regimen that produces a lifestyle of positivity, which establishes you as an asset to any relationship you encounter. You must divorce the junk you've been feeding yourself and feed on vital truths and affirmations that boost the power of what's in your heart and spirit over your cravings and emotions.

Chapter 5:

"Rehab"

For most women, being vulnerable is the scariest but most needed place in a relationship. We claim men only want sex, but my research proves that gender plays no part in sexual drive; both men and women experience the same amount of urges, which vary according to personalities. Men want women to be open, soft, exposed, honest, cooperative, receptive, surrendered and vulnerable, which men can only receive while he's engaged in sexual activity. Outside of that, most women are argumentative, jealous, closed minded, bossy, and in the extremely vulgar and abusive. Being argumentative, too aggressive, inflexible, testy, and guarded will only get you a man who will take what he can and run. Then we're left feeling inadequate and questioning our physical appearance when the problem all started with a simple miss-step: honesty; not only with him but with ourselves. When you find a "great fit", be honest and communicate the truth. Be vulnerable and allow him to lead. There is no reason why you need complete control of the relationship, simply control your reactions.

Although I am a bit of a traditionalist regarding the structure of 'family', I've never been stuck on if the man or woman should be the provider while the other is the home maker and caretaker. I believe that a relationship can last when two people are working together on what works. Some may say "easier said than done" yet, I truly believe the "magic formula" is just that simple. If the woman is the sole financial provider and the man is the caretaker or 'domestic supporter'; if it works, I say stick with it. Although our society has framed our perceptions to believe a man isn't in his rightful place if he isn't 'bringing home the bacon', I've witnessed numerous accounts where untraditional marriages have lasted longer than what we've been groomed to believe. The focus should not be the roles a man or woman plays in a relationship but recognizing the strengths and assets they bring to the union.

This doesn't warrant accepting someone without standards; it simply means to adjust your standards according to your priorities. If you want a wife or a husband, your standards should be focused more on responsibilities, prioritizing, critical thinking, problem solving skills, etc. vs. he simply has a job. A man can have an amazing job yet believe it's more important to spend his money on a flat screen television rather than invest or save. There are some who are simply looking for entertainment in relationships: 'friends with benefits' so their standards are focused on people who have more time on their hands and less to be accountable for. Our problems, Ladies, are not so much the 'type' of men we choose but our own focus of standards. Our issues begin with our own perception not his actions. Two people can see the same action at the same time and interpret or perceive it completely opposite than the other which all has to do with our own personal character and filters. There were times when I lied to myself and claimed Terrell just used me. I tried to calculate how much less time he was spending with me on the phone and justified it with a false diagnosis of 'typical manism' when the reality was his talents landed him with more jobs and he simply didn't have the down time he had before. My reactions to my own made up conditions were just regurgitated from what I practiced in past relationships. Terrell and I were never in an official serious, committed relationship. This didn't stop me from 'braking up' with him and refusing to answer his phone calls, I played "too busy to care" and responded to his texts with one word answers. I was repeating what became comfortable to me and this exposed deeper issues that he made a choice not to entertain resulting in a timeout that lasted months longer than I could stand. I'm sure by this time, he'd had enough. He only gave me honesty, friendship, passion, and authenticity, so I treated him like the men I accepted in the past; the ones who gave me lies, deception, and constant apologies.

Just like addicts going through rehabilitation, in order to achieve full sobriety we must first recognize our beliefs about our personal worth and understand the reality of what we've adopted as truth. For decades, I believed that I deserved the type of man I "saw" for myself but didn't know I was completely blinded by my past experiences and couldn't see that I sabotaged many of the encounters I had with the type of man I needed. The truth is ladies, we've never had a problem getting a man, having a man tell us he loved us and meant it, or having a real man in our lives. Our truth is that we've never opened our eyes to realize exactly what we deserved because of the men we accepted.

We must understand there are no twelve steps, tricks, potions, surgeries or products that will give us our hearts desire. Despite what the media portrays, the only thing that will unlock what you truly deserve is breaking your mind from the habits you've adopted and falling in love with your own personal truths. In love and relationships, honesty is truly the best policy and not so much for the other person but more for you. Recently, I made a choice to remain single until I was in love with all that was "me": my physical, my mental and my spiritual. I forced myself into rehab; cutting cold turkey, feeling the anguish and pains of meeting the truth. Night sweats from the fears of never having, the sickness of remembering when, and being out of control like most recovered addicts, made me feel alive. It wasn't pretty. Learning how to accept a compliment without obligation or being rejected without question was at one time foreign to me and an impossibility until my breakthrough.

"Breakthrough"

It took years. My rehab felt like the longest ever and hopelessness was my most frequent visitor. I was alone with no one to connect with. None of my friends and family understood why I made a choice to change. They became accustom to the character I portrayed for so long that they believed she was my true identity. The authentic me was someone I didn't know so I knew nothing about introducing her to others. She seemed awkward, she smiled too much and didn't hold on to the memories I moved into my emotions. She always has a rational answer for complex situations and doesn't mind being alone in silence. Most who meet her, perceive her to be the 'fake' me and at one time, I agreed. Her authenticity was something I wasn't comfortable with so demoting her made it easier to cope. But she never retreated. She grew stronger and is more beautiful than the 'me' I use to place in the mirror. The little things in life are the most important to her and she appreciates every opportunity to appear. She never feels the urge to defend herself and attracts greatness. She's warm, understanding and wise. She attracts excellence in the people around her, which exposed me to experiences I never thought possible. There were times when I could feel the 'old me' getting jealous and slipping away but I held on to her like a security blanket although my heart knew that I would need to let her go soon. I began to spend more time with this 'new me'. She stripped everything unauthentic: went out with no makeup, wore her natural hair and dressed carelessly in simple cottons that seem to be created just for her. She watched less drama on television, craves insight, and deeper education. It seems as if no matter where she appears, men and even women are attracted to her before she even speaks. She is powerful. She always holds her head high, and I can never distinguish her emotions; she cries for the unfortunate and sweats to improve. I couldn't believe this woman was genuinely me. She's recognized for the most creatively profound developments, which seem to flow from her effortlessly. I began to want to be her. I wanted to have the peace she carried and the spirit she shared without the weight of any contradicting belief. She upheld her morals and unapologetically shares her faith. The 'new me' was the identity I wanted others to see, so I began to talk like her, I practiced the way she walked and adopted her habits. She's not perfect but once I got a glimpse of her in my mirror, I preferred to reflect her authentic imperfections vs. suffering while hiding behind the 'old me'. I found security in her and didn't regret the fact that I couldn't remember the moment I released the 'old me'. I walked around as the new me so much that even those who knew me all my life acknowledged me as her. My family and friends began to fall in love with her and those who refused fell off like pedals of a dying rose that were still beneficial potpourri in our history. She and I are the best of friends and I couldn't love her any more. By definition, I would be a lesbian having her as my life partner, my better half that I want to be fruitful with and multiply. I embrace her and will fight to protect her although she's strong enough to protect herself. I am obsessed with learning more about her and every new discovery sends me into a deeper appreciation of her as a gift from God. The more intimate I am with her the more we become one and the moment I recognized that truth was the exact moment I received my breakthrough.

My breakthrough came, the moment I recognized the 'new me' is the 'me' I was created to be. Now, I have a better understanding of why fairytales and imagination are critical in a child's life; because these tales teach exploration of all of the possibilities of who you are and opens your mind to the infinite greatness available to explore. The reality is not to believe your 'prince charming' will never come but to understand that your prince will only come for his princess and will only fight to rescue the damsel who's willing. Reality is knowing regardless of how evil your stepmother is or how long you were locked in the tower, you still have the opportunity to have a happily ever after. Reality proves that no matter how society describes him as a beast, you deserve the beauty in a diamond in the rough.

As long as you play dress up and house with the characters you've rehearsed, you will never achieve all the greatness you deserve. Love is not as complicated as we profess. The complication comes when you attempt to uphold an unauthentic 'you' in reality. Your frustrations are not because of your circumstances they are the result of your refusal to acknowledge the 'true you' who has the right answers. In life, 'fake' people do not surround you; you're simply experiencing their reactions to the fake YOU. Your main challenge is releasing the security of who you are believed to be and accepting the truth of how great you really are. Your position in relationships and love have very little to do with the actions of others but more of you being accepting of their truths.

Being free from the pocket comes once you wrap yourself in authenticity and display your value above your need to be purchased. Just as a rare jewel, once your value is exhibited, those who enter your life will work for your worth, hold you close to their heart, boast about your character, take the time to secure you, and vow to keep you beyond foresight. You'll become the example of greatness in his legacy and regardless of the challenges that may arise; you will remain his precious heirloom that he will preserve until death do you part.

-Selah.

Acknowledgements

First and always grateful to GOD.

My mother: Gwendolyn D. Primous

Charterhouse Center for Families- Stockton, CA.
Mikey Kamienski, Zulema Gomez-Wimer,
April Basinger & Members of PLTI c/o 2013

Tender Hands Safe Haven- Stockton, CA.
Sharon "Cookie" Charles & Jammesie Jones

My big brother and creative advisor: "LOC LION"&
To my Big little brother Otha Mobbs.

To my Editor & little sis: Cruzita Whiteley
CTruth Potography

To: Brian, Kendrick, and Terrell thank you for your experiences that helped me become who I am today.

Shannon Christopher, Kenneth Trevillion,
Ronnie Jones, Diana Pena, Domonique McDaniels,
Marvin Tookes, and all of my supporters, family and friends.

THANK YOU.

www.ingramcontent.com/pod-product-compliance
Lightning Source LLC
Chambersburg PA
CBHW070459100426
42743CB00010B/1691